# CORPORATE

## *Wife*

# HANDBOOK

Insight and support for the role
of the Corporate Wife

# SARAH WATSON

## The Corporate Wife Handbook

First published in 2017 by

Panoma Press Ltd
48 St Vincent Drive, St Albans, Herts, AL1 5SJ, UK
info@panomapress.com
www.panomapress.com

Book layout by Neil Coe

Printed by TJ International Ltd, Padstow, Cornwall
Printed on acid-free paper from managed forests.

**ISBN 978-1-784521-05-9**

To Andrew, for inviting me into his
professional world.

To Cameron and Hamish, for being sons
that we are proud of.

To family and friends, for their love and
support.

And to Anne, for knowing that I had
"worked the room".

# Contents

# THE TIPS — 72

# THE REFLECTION — 92

# Introduction

By way of introduction, I have worked in different roles as a legal secretary for more than 25 years. My husband Andrew, a Solicitor, and I met at work at a law firm in London; I was a legal secretary, working for one of his colleagues when he joined as an Articled Clerk. We have been married for over 20 years. In that time, I have witnessed first-hand the journey and commitment that my husband and other like-minded professionals have demonstrated in order to progress and succeed within their chosen field.

The idea of creating this handbook was finally cemented by a passing comment from a good friend (and client's wife). She and her husband were guests at a corporate function, and at the end of the event, after the other guests had gone, she said that she had known I would be "working the room" that evening.

The event was a concert where my husband co-hosted a hospitality box for around 16 guests. I had spoken to everyone present, either before the performance started, or during the interval, or when the concert had finished. My friend had identified the role I needed to fulfil, knew beforehand that I was likely to fulfil it, and had watched me in action. I had indeed "worked the room", but what surprised me more was the realisation that I had done it so automatically. It had felt like the natural and normal thing to do.

This caused me to speculate that I could have been taking for granted a possible "skill" which had developed over the years – that of being a Corporate Wife. At that event, I knew I had an important role to play and understood that I needed to contribute to help create a welcoming and positive atmosphere for my husband's social business interactions. It then led me to think about the many experiences I'd had in my capacity as a Corporate Wife.

I have been fortunate to meet many charming people over the years, but have also witnessed behaviour and actions that were not quite appropriate or helpful in the corporate networking environment. It became apparent when I looked back that some people did not realise or appreciate their role in a certain situation. I hope, therefore, that this handbook will help you to reflect on the role of the Corporate Wife, help you gain the most enjoyment and positive outcomes from that role, and understand and appreciate the importance of your supportive input.

When I sent the first draft of this book to people for feedback, they raised the possibility of writing it for those in different circumstances from mine – same sex marriages, full-time husbands, full-time wives, full-time working women, full-time working men, to name but a few. Whilst everyone will have a different story to tell, and people have different circumstances in their working and private lives, I actively decided to write from my perspective. Therefore, for the purpose of this handbook, I have referred to the professional being male and the spouse being female. I acknowledge either role can be determined by either sex, and within same sex relationships, but have used this dynamic to enable a more straightforward script to relay my own experiences. I suspect that we all share the same attributes in supporting our partners, in whatever capacity, at regular times in our lives.

The feedback I received on the first draft was fascinating. I deliberately didn't send it to people who would merely pat me on the back, but to those who would give straightforward, honest views on what I had written. These views were intriguing and stimulating, and went far beyond the level of feedback I'd hoped to achieve. What I had written clearly challenged some people to reflect on their own views, circumstances, expectations and personal lifestyles. I will be equally fascinated to hear your summaries and understanding of the corporate environment, and hope this handbook will stimulate an interesting exchange of views.

Throughout this handbook I will demonstrate my thought process regarding the many different aspects of the Corporate Wife role, with explanations and considered responses. I have come to my own conclusions and viewpoints based on observing others within the corporate environment, be they positive or negative. I hope this will stimulate your own thoughts and reactions to the points I'm inviting you to consider as we all need to develop our own personal outlook on life based on our reaction to others and what happens around us.

This handbook will assist you and help you gain the most from your opportunities as a Corporate Wife. It will give you a clearer picture of what might be expected of you when attending the professional networking environment, and how your approach and reaction could have a positive or negative effect on your partner's career.

The whole topic of the Corporate Wife has so many different interpretations for people, as does their perception of their role within the corporate world – if indeed they consider themselves to be part of it. Regardless of our outlook and our opinion of the corporate environment, we all need to conduct ourselves with dignity within that environment and acknowledge that it is a different aspect of our lives where different rules apply. We need to display different behaviour and to some extent rein in some of our character traits.

When I first started my journey as a Corporate Wife, there wasn't any support telling me what that environment was like; what was expected of me; what the general code of conduct was; how to behave in a corporate networking environment. I had to learn as I went along.

Whether anyone wishes to accept or ignore the fact, there is a particular way to behave within the corporate environment. There is a level of etiquette to be aware of and demonstrate with your behaviour – not a fixed set of rules, but merely a foundation of how to conduct yourself, and why. I hope you find my experiences and insight informative.

I will demonstrate the reasons why it is important to get your role as a Corporate Wife right and how it could in some way affect your husband's professional standing if you get it wrong. It will at times be a demanding journey, but on another level, it's one that enables you to make a valuable contribution, experience stunning venues and meet interesting people who will enrich and entertain you.

# My Background

On leaving school, I wanted the quickest route into work so I enrolled on a one-year secretarial course at college. In those days, there were so many jobs available, and I knew secretarial work offered a good salary within the legal or medical profession.

My first job was close to home, working at a law firm in Bromley, Kent, to gain experience; but I knew I ultimately wanted to work in London. After a few years of working locally, I made the move to London where my first job was at the law firm my now husband was soon to join as a Trainee Solicitor.

An "office relationship" wasn't easy, but it was a relatively small firm and we both conducted ourselves in a professional manner at work. We informed the Senior Partner of our relationship, but didn't bring it to the attention of any colleagues for some time. In fact, the level of our discretion gained my husband the easiest £20 he has ever earned.

A large group from the office had decamped to the local pub after work. During the evening, a fellow Trainee Solicitor had a mischievous bet that Andrew couldn't persuade me to leave the pub with him. Andrew told me of the bet, pretending to the colleague that he had simply offered me one of his best chat-up lines. I still recall the amazed look on our colleague's face when, 10 minutes later, I gave Andrew a cheeky grin then walked out of the pub with him.

Once our relationship was out in the open, it took the colleague many months to forgive us for our deception. It took me longer to forgive the colleague for suggesting the bet in the first place!

As our relationship was becoming more serious, Andrew reached the stage in his career where he was being considered for partnership. That coincided with the natural time for me to move to a different law firm so I could continue freely with my own career as he began the next stage of his journey up the corporate ladder.

I worked for many years as a legal secretary to Senior Partner level, earning a respectable wage along the way. After a few years of marriage, I made the decision, with Andrew's agreement, to stop working in London and find a job closer to home in Guildford, Surrey. This allowed us time to adjust to the decrease in my salary before we started a family. We didn't want to deal with a large decrease in income at the same time as the large increase in expenditure inevitable when raising and supporting children.

Andrew has continued to juggle his professional and private life, and I have had a varied and busy life too. Whilst raising our two boys, I have had various paid jobs as well as voluntary and charity roles. I have also found the time to get involved with supporting our boys' schools, helping at their social or fundraising events. So my life has many different aspects to it – as is the case for the majority of people.

Being a Corporate Wife has always been *one* aspect of my life. Sometimes it has taken on a more dominant role; sometimes it has been in the background. But it has always remained a part of my life rather than defining who I am or what is expected of me. Nonetheless, for the purpose of supporting Andrew on his professional journey, it has always been important that I understand and perform the role when needed to the best of my ability.

# The "Skill" and the Title

If being a Corporate Wife can be regarded as a skill, we need a definition of what that "skill" is.

To me, there are many aspects to the Corporate Wife skill. It is having the ability to step into any corporate event or environment and respond to your surroundings in an appropriate manner. It is knowing how important your attendance is to your partner in order to support his efforts to succeed.

The purpose of the corporate event will likely be one of two: to enable your husband to make new business connections; or to acknowledge, develop and continue established connections. Your attendance at the event is a way of showing that you know the event matters to him, and that you are willing to stand beside him.

Everyone's career is of importance – it finances all aspects of their personal lives, be they practical or leisure. Ultimately the support you give to your partner in his endeavour to succeed will, no doubt, be returned to you. Let's not lose sight of the fact that it works both ways.

Every person needs support with their endeavours, but the focus in this handbook is supporting a professional partner. You can combine your life with the demands of being a Corporate Wife – I have not yet come across anyone who says their Corporate Wife duty takes over their life. Rather it is one part of the overall picture.

It is an honourable skill to know when to support your partner actively, when to stand back, when to keep things ticking along smoothly in the background, and when to stand by his side. From witnessing a variety of behaviours within the corporate environment over many years, and the positive or negative effect they've created, I would argue that it is a vital skill to understand what is expected of you and act accordingly. Knowing how to act within a professional networking setting is important. Interacting with people who are coming together because of their business connections is different to interacting with people for purely social reasons.

Within the corporate networking environment, you as a Corporate Wife are attending to help create, build and cement business relationships, not personal relationships, and that is why corporate etiquette matters. You need to understand the unspoken rules: how to respond and react to people (some of whom may be complete strangers to you); how to conduct yourself and make the connection. You are not in your normal, familiar environment; your purpose is to support your professional partner and his efforts to succeed. You don't have to "hard sell" yourself, or try to be heard, or voice your opinion. You do not try to promote your partner, either. It is *his* environment in which to perform, to succeed, to network, to create a strong professional image. You are there to support; to back-up; to make the effort for your loved one.

So how would you describe the term "Corporate Wife"? Is it a necessary or relevant title?

Professionals have to work incredibly hard, showing consistent commitment and energy towards their chosen profession. That journey is made better and easier with a supportive partner. Being a Corporate Wife is not a calling, or a career path, or a deliberate choice; it is a way of describing a person who gives support to their professional partner.

It is peculiar to think that most people are aware of the role of the Corporate Wife yet nobody claims to be one. Nobody seems to define the role, and nobody that I can think of is recognised as being a Corporate Wife. Whilst writing this book, I have reached the conclusion that being a Corporate Wife is a term that describes one aspect of my life when I am effectively "on duty" for my husband. Within the corporate environment, we Corporate Wives have a role to play and a job to do.

When I received early feedback from my first draft, some people disagreed with the title. Others could not quite decide upon its definition. Some people actively dislike titles. Others need the identity of a title. The outlook I demonstrate in this handbook is one perspective which will hopefully elicit your own views.

The whole idea of a "title" doesn't actually affect me either way. Ultimately, it is a personal choice whether a title is relevant to you. If your confidence is boosted by a title, that is perfectly acceptable. If it has no relevance to you, that's fine too. Different views are what make life so fascinating, stimulating us to find our own boundaries and opinions. Whether you feel indifference or admiration for those who work within the corporate environment, there *is* a code of conduct which makes everyone's professional career run as smoothly as possible.

# Personal Relationships

I will only briefly touch on this topic to give you an all-round viewpoint of the life you will likely lead, and the expectations of you in your capacity as a Corporate Wife. I am not seeking to advise you on how to progress personal relationships as my focus is to offer help and guidance for your role in the corporate environment.

In the majority of cases, when people's paths first cross they are both deeply involved in the early stages of their careers. They have the energy, enthusiasm and drive to succeed and climb their career ladder. They are earning their own income, fully engaged by their chosen path, and feel that every opportunity is theirs for the taking.

Corporate professionals tend to be driven and hardworking from the outset. They will probably have an idea of where they are heading in their professional capacity, the time it will take to get there, key individuals who will help them on that journey, and where they want to be in say 10, 15, 20 years time. If you enter into a relationship with someone of that nature, chances are they will be looking for similar attributes in you, too.

They may consider, as the relationship develops, whether you are the right person to go on the corporate journey with them.

Professionals are drawn to, and used to dealing with, energetic, focused, hardworking people. They will not be attracted to nervous, hesitant people – those traits don't survive in a corporate environment, so the professional will not look for them in their partner either. That is not to suggest you need to be bullish and driven, but the professional is unlikely to have the time or inclination to interact with you if you are needy.

Is there a strong argument that says people are attracted to those who have the same outlook and energy as them? Isn't that an obvious starting point? If you are, for example, an active person who likes outdoor leisure pursuits, it's unlikely that you will be attracted to a person who prefers staying in, watching TV.

When we make those first connections with a partner, they are normally built on common ground. The relationship develops as we have a level of understanding of each other's outlook, interests, values, viewpoints – those are the core points that draw us together. If a professional person is driven and focused, their partner will need to understand and accept that.

When Andrew and I first met, I was already working in the legal environment so I knew the level of commitment that he and others in that profession had to demonstrate in order to succeed. Did that make it easier to connect? Maybe, but that wasn't the only factor.

My dad had his own business, and my mum combined raising myself and my two brothers with part-time work, so I have always understood the simple fact that in order to succeed, I'd need to put in effort. As I have mainly been involved in the legal environment throughout my working life, I do wonder if different professions need different levels of drive (and support) to succeed. But I would nonetheless argue that it would ultimately come back to the same level of connection and understanding in order for a personal relationship to develop. You will have your own ambitions for your career and lifestyle, and you will no doubt connect with your partner if you have a similar approach, regardless of the particular profession.

# Professional Relationships

Strong client/corporate relationships are the key to successful careers for every professional. People simply cannot progress without strong working connections within their chosen field.

As they begin the corporate journey, people learn from their peers in the company how to respond to clients with whom they wish to interact. From day one, the professional will discover what is expected of him.

The senior members of his working team will expect effort, commitment, integrity and confidence. His peers will expect support, teamwork, diplomacy and skill. The clients will expect understanding, support, connection and dedication.

Every working relationship is important, from the team around him to the opportunities offered by his clients. From day one, the professional will consider what he himself can offer and deliver, what people alongside him are offering and delivering, what his competitor is offering and delivering, and how his chosen field is progressing in order to progress alongside and within it. His success is determined by his professional skills and relationships. His understanding of his surroundings, as well as his connection to other professionals and their expectations along with the ability to deliver the required standard of skill and knowledge, influences his progression up the corporate ladder. This is true of any person, in any profession.

Every professional conducts himself within the boundaries of the corporate environment in which he is working. He will have to understand the task ahead of him, defining the goals he wants to achieve and the route he needs to take to obtain that success.

We all meet a variety of people on our journey through life. Some will be similar to us, others will have different outlooks, different approaches and different logic. But the end goal tends to be the same: we all want a successful life, whether success for us is defined as being financially secure, happy, content, surrounded by love or surrounded by material gain. Whatever our goals may be, ultimately we want our efforts to translate into our individual perception of success.

Professionals recognise the people who will have a positive effect on their ambitions. They will develop working relationships with those people and invest their time and energy to create corporate connections. That does not necessarily translate into a strong personal connection with another person in the corporate environment – professionals come together through the common ground of their particular profession and the benefit that they will all gain from working together.

When people come together for business reasons, they have to conduct themselves with corporate etiquette. They need to respect the mutual support and the level of knowledge that each party can bring to the working relationship. After all, they are coming together for a specific reason: a shared interest in their professional field.

That is why the Corporate Wife needs to understand the logic and necessity behind the interaction: that the corporate networking environment is the place to cement business relationships. She also needs to acknowledge the connection that the professional parties have with one another.

Every professional performs his role with a duty of care in order to achieve his success. If you, as a Corporate Wife, understand and respect his drive and ambition to succeed, you are more likely to help make that corporate journey work. If the professional does not have the necessary support on both a personal and professional level, his efforts to succeed will be more likely to falter or even fail. By acknowledging the importance of the professional relationships for your partner with the effort you make, you will help him achieve his goals, which will ultimately reward both of you for all the hard work and commitment. You are a part of the jigsaw that helps to create his success.

# Early Days

When my husband was in the early stages of his career as a Solicitor, he was travelling to a meeting to give legal advice on a high-value corporate deal, the biggest transaction he had been instructed on at that point in his career. The client was very senior within his organisation, well-regarded within the industry, and a business force to be reckoned with.

As they travelled to the meeting, the client stared at my husband, pointed a finger at him, and said, "Are you lucky?"

My husband immediately responded with a firm, "Yes!" Then the general conversation continued until they reached the meeting venue. The meeting was a huge success, with my husband gaining a far better deal than the client had anticipated, and a career-long relationship was born.

The same client, some time later, enquired about me. He said to my husband, "To support you, she's either very pushy or very laid-back."

My husband relayed this comment to me, to my amusement. Soon after, I happened to meet the client at a corporate event. After a brief exchange, he turned to my husband and said, "I'm glad to see she is the latter." I have met the client on many occasions since, and I am happy to say that his business relationship with Andrew has gone from strength to strength.

There is no assumption on my part that I created the bond between my husband and that client. This story merely demonstrates that, without doubt, the Corporate Wife helps to cement corporate relationships, completing the picture the client perceives of the professional. Professionals need to trust and respect one another, and the Corporate Wife's demeanour and behaviour can help to build that trust.

If I had come across as a pushy person, the client may have considered that I was too much of a driving force behind my husband, and that Andrew was trying to further his professional career with the added pressure of my high expectations of him. If I came across as laid-back – which, fortunately, I clearly did – then the client knew my husband was pursuing the business connection based on his own eagerness to progress and achieve, without any conditions or pressure from me.

Focusing for a moment on the point about the supportive partner being laid-back or pushy, I'm not saying either is wrong or right. You work as a partnership in a way that suits both of you, and brings out the best in both of you. Some professionals need a pushy person standing behind them; they wouldn't get anything done otherwise. They may be quite capable, but still need that nudge. Some people need a laid-back person standing behind them as they want to get on with their professional life without their partner giving input. Regardless of whether you are pushy or laid-back, strong willed or easy-going, the same set of corporate etiquette rules apply when supporting a professional partner.

As your personal relationship becomes more serious, you start on the corporate journey with your partner. You will have to understand and accept the late nights, deadlines and demanding workload. On reflection, I was not called upon too often in the early days of my husband's career (my "visual" role started when he was at Senior Assistant level). The early stage was his time to prove himself within his chosen field, so my role as Corporate Wife was more important behind the scenes. I will demonstrate this with another anecdote in the following chapter.

# Assistant Level

My husband and a colleague were working late towards the completion date of another deal. They had both been working through the night regularly, only coming home to shower and get fresh clothing, sometimes catching a quick nap at their desks to maximise time working on the transaction.

With another full night ahead of them, both men called their respective partners to let us know they wouldn't be home that night. As he arrived home the next day,

Andrew gave me a heartfelt hug. When he'd called me to explain his fate, I had offered nothing but support, asking if he wanted me to track down a late night food delivery company in the vicinity of their office so he and his colleague could keep their energy levels up.

The Corporate Wife needs to recognise the pressure that professionals are under and never add to them, regardless of how distressed she herself may be feeling. Some might say that Corporate Wives have the right to stick up for themselves and expect the company and time of their spouse, rather than conducting themselves in a subservient manner. My response would be that the professional must have drive, ambition, and energy to succeed, and *that will continue* as they progress with their career. There is nothing wrong with being supportive and understanding towards another person, and I suspect most professionals would agree that their working life is helped immensely when they do have the support and understanding of their partner.

Let's look at the situation from a totally different angle. Imagine if I had yelled abuse down the phone when Andrew called me, furious that I was spending another evening without him and expressing my disgust at his decision in no uncertain terms. Imagine if as a result he had then said to the client, who had a major corporate deal about to close, "Sorry – I'm going home early as I haven't seen my wife." The client, quite simply, would have moved on to the next professional who puts their business needs first.

Let's be in no doubt: being a Corporate Wife does come at a cost. You are likely to be deprived of time with your partner from day one. There has been many an evening when I've had no contact from my husband. There have been many meals I've prepared and binned as he went out for supper with a client at short notice. But that is corporate life. Be aware of that fact, and ask yourself whether you can cope with it.

Let's say you are not seeing much of your partner, and it is beginning to nag at you. You raise your concerns with him, he listens and actively comes home earlier and more regularly. You have more time together and life feels good. Then one day he tells you his colleagues are getting more work than him, or that a job he pitched for has gone to a competitor, or that others who joined the firm at the same time as him are being considered for promotion, and he isn't. It happens.

The skill as a Corporate Wife is in understanding your husband's profession, what he wants to achieve, what he *has to do* to achieve that, and the knock-on effect it will have on you as a couple.

This handbook is not meant to be negative, or portray gloom and doom. I am simply offering you a perspective, putting it to you that your relationship with a professional is more likely to succeed if you accept the commitment he has to make to his work environment. The upside is not only the increased likelihood of financial stability, but also the experiences you can have beyond your day-to-day life, the people you will meet in the corporate environment, the venues and events you will experience, and the simple pleasure of being around people who take every opportunity to reward their own effort and hard work.

It is likely that whilst your partner is in the early stages of his professional career, you will be too. You will both be working, steadily making your mark in your chosen field, so remind yourself that his professional efforts at this stage reflect your own, and that it is beneficial to you both to show support for each other.

Whilst working at assistant level, a professional has plenty of drive, energy and ambition. They are finally putting into practice their background and training. They want to take on every business proposition that crosses their path. If you are like-minded, you will understand that energy and drive. If you are less driven, you will need to understand their motives and incentives in order to support them fully.

I was not as driven as Andrew, but that did not lessen my understanding of what he wanted to achieve. I was quite happy moving along beside him, pursuing my own career as well as enjoying relationships with family and friends, and pursuing hobbies and interests, with or without him. The key for me was that I understood from an early stage that Andrew had to make a strong commitment to his career in order to succeed. I didn't question it; I didn't challenge it; I didn't disagree with it.

I simply understood it.

If you understand that outlook, the chances are you will be capable of providing the support your professional partner needs, and will hopefully see the role of Corporate Wife as a beneficial addition to your life.

# Marriage

As a couple's careers stabilise and they start to achieve their professional targets (for example, building up their client base, progressing within their company), this tends to be the stage of life where they decide to make a commitment to one another. The professional is establishing himself as experienced in his field, so he has a window of opportunity to consider other aspects of his life.

As a couple's relationship becomes more serious when one partner is a professional, it is a good idea for both of them to consider the long-term lifestyle – I'm not referring to the material side of things, but rather the emotional commitment and the journey they will embark upon together.

When you enter into the commitment of marriage, you are acknowledging a connection. The professional's ambition to succeed will not decrease once you are married, so you need to commit to marriage whilst being fully aware of his duty to different aspects of his own life as well as the life you create together. You probably want him to support you in all of your working and leisure pursuits, so surely that works in return.

If you are talking about making a commitment to your partner through marriage, but you have concerns about the demands of his profession, it is crucial that you discuss your concerns openly and honestly. The marriage will hopefully be a mutually pleasant journey through many years of happy life together, so it will not be a good starting point if you enter into it with any resentment over the dedication he has to show to his profession. Any professional, in any industry, has to work long, demanding hours in order to succeed. If you understand this from the outset, there is a greater chance you can work together as a team, which is what both people in a relationship will want and need. As my recollection in the previous chapter demonstrated, it led to a far better outcome for both my husband and myself that I responded with patience and understanding.

Please be reminded that the purpose of this handbook is to give you a viewpoint on supporting your professional partner. It is *one* aspect of my life that I have chosen to focus on. Other aspects of your life won't stop when you take on the role of Corporate Wife; you add the role of Corporate Wife to your existing life, and work around it as you do with everything else. I am not asking you to hero worship the professional, be the perfect wife, or put his needs first; I am simply putting it to you that he will succeed to a far greater level with your support.

# Having a Family

Given our modern society and the fact that people's outlooks are continually changing, there is now a wide variety of family dynamics to consider. Despite these changes, with the majority of people that I have come across in the corporate environment, the biggest responsibility for the parenting role still appears to be with the female in relationships.

I have seen many women, over many years, lessen their work commitment or stop working completely to look after their family. It is an issue that is debated to this day, along with the other related topics such as equal pay, equality in business etc.

There are advantages and disadvantages, logic and circumstances, for every decision we make in life. Decisions can be based on want or need. You may not want to decrease your efforts with your own career, but you may need to in order to look after your family. You may not want to juggle family life with demanding working hours, but you may need to if you want that professional success, or have financial obligations. Ultimately, it's down to you.

Could it be said that decisions based on need count as doing something for others? Is a decision based on want, more personal? In my capacity as a Corporate Wife, I decided to support my husband based on need rather than want, but that doesn't devalue the importance of my role. I need and want to support my professional partner, because he needs me to.

If you are married to a professional, he will be investing a huge amount of time to succeed in his profession. The balance of any relationship varies, but it is a great compliment that your husband trusts and respects you enough to take on the huge role of raising the family. You in turn compliment him by trusting and respecting him to do what he needs to do in a professional capacity, to keep you all financially secure.

As I have mentioned previously, I cannot speak for people in relationships where both partners give a strong commitment to their professional life. I simply don't know how they share their responsibilities. Ultimately, you have to decide as a couple what works for you; there is never one rule for all.

Whilst you may hope that your professional husband will be a consistently hands-on father, please remember his starting point. He is driven and passionate about his profession, focused on where he wants to be in his career, and the steps he has to take to get there. He will know whom he needs to impress with his professional knowledge, and needs to decide instinctively when the time is right to progress to the next level of his career.

He will probably look at the family situation quite simply. Once you have created a family together, it will only increase the emphasis that he puts on himself to succeed in a business capacity, as he now has to provide for and support his family. His drive and ambition will have cranked up a few notches.

I remember attending a Partners' Conference with my husband, where a good number of spouses were in attendance too. Whilst we (the spouses) were sitting in the hotel lobby, relaxing and socialising, a gentleman walked through the lobby pushing a pram.

At this point, one wife remarked, "There's no way he's one of our lot – he's actually pushing the pram!" The laughter that broke out in the group suggested that we were all in agreement with her assessment.

We were incredibly fortunate that we could cope financially when I stopped working to raise our boys. I quite understand this is not the same for everyone, and indeed that many people wish to continue with their careers whilst raising their family. No one needs to justify their actions. The key to success is how you work with your partner, to achieve the life and outlook that suits and complements you both.

# Senior Level

So all the years of commitment, long hours and lack of sleep are finally paying off. Your husband has reached the senior level within his profession. But it doesn't stop there.

His job is now to maintain that level of success with his professional approach and continue to respond to professional demands with the skill he has shown thus far, justifying and confirming his rise through the ranks. I would argue that this is probably his most demanding phase on the basis that he still has to perform with a high level of care and attention, but without the first flush of youth on his side to counteract the ongoing lack of downtime.

His working task list could now include:

- maintaining his own reputation in his profession,

- helping assistants to progress through the ranks,

- working successfully with the established client base,

- maintaining the top level of service to the clients,

- becoming involved with the internal management side of the business.

You can probably see why he might feel a little worn out now and then.

My recollection is that my "visual" role as Corporate Wife started when my husband got to Senior Assistant level, and has continued as he maintains the senior level of his career. Whilst raising our children, running the home, organising our social life and my work schedule, I found myself adding Corporate Entertaining to my "To Do" list.

When I use the term "Corporate Entertaining", I mean it collectively – in other words, as a corporate host or corporate guest. When your partner reaches senior level, corporate entertaining takes place either to maintain existing business relationships or create new ones. Both reasons are equally crucial to the continued success of the professional.

By the time your partner is entertaining at senior level, it is likely that he will be well-known to his colleagues and clients in a business capacity, and to some extent in a personal capacity too. If you consider the amount of time professionals spend communicating with each other, it is understandable that they will get to know one another on a more personal level.

After many years in his profession, Andrew is fully aware of the different character traits and expectations of people he meets in a business capacity. He knows the level of care and attention that each client needs, both in relation to his time and expertise, and their preference for the type of corporate networking event, and he will respond to that knowledge accordingly.

To put that into context, if Andrew wishes to entertain an important client and knows that client doesn't care much for, say, opera, is Andrew likely to buy tickets for Wagner's *Ring Cycle*? Of course not! In his corporate capacity, he has to demonstrate the correct etiquette to complement the business connection.

Imagine you have to attend a theatre performance in your capacity as a Corporate Wife, but you actually saw the same performance the previous week. What do you do? Corporate etiquette would suggest that you attend the second time without question, as this time you are attending in your role as Corporate Wife to support your husband; you are there for corporate networking reasons, not for your personal leisure. If you let slip that you saw the performance only days ago, the corporate etiquette would be to add that you enjoyed it so much, you are happy to see it again.

One question I was often asked in the early feedback from this handbook was how I choose and book restaurants or venues for corporate entertaining. That is something I have rarely had to do myself; it is not the Corporate Wife's responsibility. The reason for the corporate event is to enhance business connections, and the Corporate Wife's role is to support her partner, not organise the event.

As a Corporate Wife, you will either be the wife of the host, or the wife of a guest. In the corporate environment, the invitation is not personal to you; it's in response to the relevance of your professional partner within that working community. The only situation that comes to mind where I would be involved with the decision making is when we are hosting dinner at home, or possibly when hosting a more personal dinner reservation (say, for one client and his wife). If Andrew needs to impress the client and his wife, I may give him my thoughts in relation to the potential venue, but ultimately he will be the one to choose a suitable location. If we are hosting dinner at home, we will discuss how we can create a menu that will demonstrate a little more effort than usual, or if the event is to be more relaxed, we may invite the client and his wife for "supper" rather than "dinner".

To some extent, corporate entertaining is a little easier for the professional when he reaches senior level. His business contacts are established so the majority of networking events will be with people he is familiar with, and probably you are too. If the senior level corporate entertaining is to secure new business contacts, it is likely that the networking will be taking place because the potential client has heard of your partner's business reputation and wishes to create a relationship with him. And vice versa – your husband may feel the potential client is a business connection worth getting to know.

# Partners' Conferences

I would like to touch on the subject of Partners' Conferences. I have attended different conferences with Andrew over the years, which has enabled me to stay in beautiful surroundings for a few precious days, all of which have been a pleasant escape from the daily routine.

Conferences are organised to create an opportunity for colleagues, who have the common bond of their profession, to come together. With busy working lives, these conferences are at times the only opportunity that professionals have to properly interact, especially if they are based in different offices or even different countries.

The main purpose of the conference is to cement professional development and to use that precious and rare time away from the office wisely, to communicate with each other.

A firm might acknowledge wives and their support of the professional, by accepting their attendance at the conference venue, and in some cases that tends to be the extent of the wives' invitation. Some firms alternatively offer a "Spouse Programme". I personally have always enjoyed joining Andrew at those conferences which do not provide that option – considering the demands of day-to-day life, the prospect of a few days of relaxation is far more appealing to me than being told what to do, when and where.

I recall one conference in particular. The professionals had been in meetings all day and were due to attend the main gala evening. I met another wife in the hotel lobby just before the scheduled start time of the conference drinks reception. We agreed to have a stroll around the hotel grounds, whereupon we came across the area designated for the drinks reception. It was elegant, with tables beautifully laid out, the shimmer from the hotel swimming pool throwing light across the vast veranda, which in turn overlooked the sea. The whole scene was complimented by the background noise of breaking waves. It was stunning.

We were then approached by a gentleman, who started talking to us. As the firm had many offices, we assumed he was based in a different location from our husbands. We made small talk, but became aware of the time and knew the conference attendees were due to arrive at any minute – and we were on their patch. As the time became apparent, the gentleman then volunteered that he was a normal guest staying at the hotel, that his wife was upstairs in their room with a headache, and that he had just wandered down to have a look around.

Panic set in, as neither myself nor the other wife wanted to be found in the allocated space for the conference guests, so we said our farewells to the gentleman, and beat a hasty retreat before we were spotted. We both understood that it was not our place to be in the midst of the conference venue. If our husbands had arrived at that point and seen us, they would have wondered what we were up to. If our husbands' colleagues had arrived, they would have noticed two wives potentially about to join their event. Myself and the other wife both understood the boundaries, and did not want to be seen as crossing them.

Whilst the majority of wives understood those boundaries, and indeed embraced the opportunity to relax and unwind, others have shown different interpretations of the event.

Looking back, some wives just could not accept they were not included in any part of the conference programme. Some openly and defiantly gate-crashed events. Some lurked in the background until they caught their partner's eye. It was, at times, like taking a front row seat watching a comedy of errors. I can remember wives crouching behind hedges, waving their arms frantically, some of whom were noticed by the majority of the conference attendees, but not their actual husbands!

Those wives did not understand the corporate etiquette. The Partners' Conference was not the wives platform to seek attention. As wives, we were in attendance purely at the discretion of our husbands, as a personal gesture of gratitude for our support. If those wives managed to persuade their professional partners to leave the conference activity, was there a risk that the professional's colleagues would have noticed? How would that have come across to his colleagues? If the wife was determined to coax him away, did that mean the professional did not consider it important to give his working environment his full attention?

# What About You?

Here's the point where you champion yourself, and everything you have done, achieved, and hope to do in the future. How will your list of achievements affect and influence your partner's corporate networking success?

It won't, really.

You are not defined by the role of Corporate Wife. You are defined by your values, your connection to others, and your outlook on life.

Whilst I gave you some of my background earlier in the book, I did not go into detail about who I am… because I don't need to.

This is an important point to make in relation to your role as a Corporate Wife. You will attend corporate networking events to support your professional partner. People will no doubt show an interest in you as it's normal human nature, but your background, outlook and lifestyle will not affect your partner's success within his chosen field. In your capacity of Corporate Wife, you complete the picture of who other professionals perceive your partner to be. Professionals do not work together based upon whether they like each other's wives – it is built on mutual respect and trust in each other's professional ability.

So as a Corporate Wife, you are there in a supportive role. The corporate world is not the environment for you to be noticed or heard. That does not belittle anything you have done or achieved, or value deeply. It means that you value the commitment your husband must show to his profession just as much as you value every other aspect of his and your life.

Do you really need your husband's networking environment to acknowledge you, who you are and what you stand for? If you work, would you not find it a little strange if your husband escorted you to your business event, and then spent the evening talking about his own business achievements? There's a time and a place, as the phrase goes.

Too often I have seen spouses attend corporate events and hand over their own business cards, regardless of whether they are in completely different fields of work and have no potential of connecting with the networking professionals in attendance. I beg you – don't belittle your own profession by trying to make your mark at your partner's event. Keep it as a topic for discussion – self-promoting will likely not bear you any fruit, and the people in attendance will not regard your behaviour as correct corporate etiquette.

# Corporate Entertaining

Corporate entertaining covers a huge range of situations and experiences: lunches, suppers, concerts, plays, leisure activities, sporting events – the list goes on. Through attending corporate events with Andrew, I have without doubt had opportunities to enjoy experiences and meet people I probably would not have had through other aspects of my life.

When I am juggling the needs of family, friends, careers and leisure time, it takes focused effort to find time to organise everything, so corporate entertaining is a welcome bonus, enabling me to attend a huge range of creative events, dine in fantastic settings, and meet a fascinating variety of people. I hope you will encounter similar experiences, as I have found them to be an interesting and enjoyable addition to my life.

I am aware, however, that some people find corporate entertaining a chore. Some wives refuse to get involved; others attend, but find it incredibly difficult to feel at ease in the environment. Of course, in contrast there are those who embrace every opportunity, openly enjoying the fact that the experience hasn't been financed by their own personal wallet (which is *not* proper corporate etiquette, by the way).

Whatever the nature of the corporate entertaining, first and foremost it has been organised to bring together professional people. The event or venue has been chosen by the host always with a business motive behind the choice.

Let's say, for example, that the invitation is to a restaurant. You might have been there many times, you may not particularly like the food, but if you are invited to join your husband, attend graciously. The only reason I have ever attended any corporate event in my capacity as Corporate Wife is quite simply because I am Andrew's wife.

Your husband may from time to time feel it appropriate to decline a corporate invitation for reasons relating to business, even if he is aware that the venue has always been on your own personal "tick list". If your husband feels it necessary to decline the invitation, his priority is to consider the benefit of the networking event for business purposes.

When Andrew and I attend corporate events, I always make sure that "domestic" arrangements are in place. By that, I mean that I've covered any personal workload to allow for the time spent at and travelling to the event. I organise home arrangements to allow for any unexpected delays or overrunning of events, and even carry out simple chores in advance to help with the smooth running of the day *after*. Corporate events can be tiring as you are on your "best behaviour", so it helps to lessen the load for the following day.

Trustworthy childcare, where relevant, is important too. When our boys were younger, this included making sure in advance that the babysitter could stay on longer if the event overran. As our boys got older, the main responsibility was to make sure the fridge was full and that their homework was at least underway before I left home. When attending the corporate event, I could then concentrate on it and give it the required levels of time and attention, knowing that other aspects of my life were covered.

You can normally get an idea of the type of corporate event from the invitation or venue itself. The internet is a great tool to use if you are invited to a restaurant that you haven't been to before. If you look beforehand at the restaurant's website and sample menu, that will give you an indication of its style. You can gauge from the type of food on the menu whether the event will be formal or relaxed – if there is something on the menu that you can't pronounce or haven't seen on the supermarket shelf, the chances are that the event will be formal.

If time permits beforehand, I ask Andrew who will be attending the event and any background he can give me, such as an idea of the event's timing and whether it could run over, what his connection is to the people we will be spending time with, how much he currently works with those people, etc. If you can have a quick chat about the event beforehand, then you will have an insight into what your husband hopes to achieve by attending.

Putting that into context, if Andrew advises me that the event is to celebrate a recent deal, I know it is likely that the people attending will be relaxed, celebratory and informal. Conversely, if the event is to impress potential new clients, the atmosphere will be more formal, business-focused and polite.

As time goes on, you will become familiar with the consistent business contacts that your husband has, together with their outlook and behaviour within the professional networking environment. For some time, I have found I am able to gauge how long the event will last, whether it will be formal or informal, and whether it could continue past the invitation schedule based on the "accepted" guest list. You will, without doubt, gain that skill too.

I will finish this section by concentrating on the point about events overrunning. It is an important point to consider, as events rarely run to schedule. Also, they tend to create such a good atmosphere that attendees wish to continue beyond the given timings.

In the early days of corporate entertaining, I would give our babysitter a clear idea of when we expected to return home. I also regularly had to sneak away from the group to call the babysitter, asking if he/she could stay at our home longer, so there came a point where I arranged the childcare to continue way past the scheduled finishing time. Then Andrew and I could relax and enjoy the event. There was no need for me to call and negotiate with the babysitter to stay later, and all concerned were happy and understood the arrangement.

# Before Arriving

Having your home life in place, and a trusted family member or child minder staying there if you have young children, helps you to relax and focus on the corporate event. If older children know where you are and what you are doing, it helps them understand what is happening, your timings and their responsibilities in your absence.

Check your travel times and the location of the venue beforehand, then you will be able to schedule your day and decide when you will have to start your journey in order to arrive on time. Please don't leave it until the last minute – it is poor corporate etiquette to arrive late at a function, which in turn will create stress for you and your husband. Gauge the potential time spent away from your work and find a way to make up that time either before or after the event. All of these points are logical, but they're essential to consider to help you feel more calm and engaged with the corporate event.

It is very important to arrive feeling calm and engaged at the event, so even if you are running late, a visit to the "Ladies" *before* you arrive at the venue is a good idea. Imagine the scene – your husband has established a strong relationship with an important client; there is mutual trust; they can see many years of a strong solid business relationship ahead. To seal the deal they are coming together socially with their wives, and then you arrive, only to charge through the venue to find the toilet. Make yourself comfortable, and you will arrive in the correct mindset.

Another tip is to have "just in case" items in your handbag. As well as usual items such as your purse and keys, consider carrying things like spare tights, loose change, nail file, tampons/sanitary towels, blister plasters, headache tablets – the list could go on. You don't want to arrive with a small suitcase under your arm, but considering any minor hitches is always a good call.

For example, I am an expert at snagging tights with my fingernails, so there is usually a spare pair tucked at the bottom of my bag. Even if you don't use any of the items, someone you are socialising with may need them, thereby providing you with the opportunity to support them with a quick solution – an especially good idea when your husband is the host.

Regardless of how busy your day is, and the fact that you may be running behind schedule to get to the corporate event in time, make sure you have a light snack before you attend. If you have a rough idea of the schedule, you may know what time you can expect to eat, but so many corporate events start with socialising over a drink, and if you are drinking on an empty stomach that could spell disaster for the time ahead. Even if you, like me, don't drink alcohol, if you forget to eat something before the event starts, you could be utterly charming and sociable, but your stomach rumbles won't be. A light snack will keep hunger at bay and lessen the effect of alcohol on an empty stomach, especially if the event is running behind schedule, and it's doubtful that it will ruin any meal offered at the event.

# First Impressions

When you walk into the room, persuade yourself to demonstrate "presence". By that, I mean behave as if you are entitled to be there, that you have a reason for being there – because you do!

Don't walk in and head for the nearest corner. Convince yourself to act confidently, as if you are relaxed and at ease in that environment. Believe you can have an enjoyable evening.

Your starting point is that your husband wants you to be there, he wants you to interact with his colleagues and clients, and he wants them to get to know you as well. After many years of walking into new environments, I take the view that if I look relaxed and confident, my mind may well follow that lead.

At a corporate event, the professionals have naturally got the head-start. They will know (or know of) at least half the people in the room when they walk in. If you and your husband get the chance to discuss the event beforehand, you can gain an idea of who is important to him, who is influential, whom he needs to impress, and whom he is hoping to interact with during the event.

Don't forget – you will be in the same position as the other Corporate Wives in the room when you walk in. None of you know what to expect; you don't know how the event will progress, whether it will be formal or fun, or the type of people that you will meet.

It is within everyone's capability to make the event work or fall flat. If you feel absolutely petrified, let your partner know before the event. Once you are both in attendance, he will have to focus on networking, regardless of how formal or relaxed the event is. If you've let him know beforehand that you are anxious, he can then support you and give you some useful information, such as who will be present, whom you are likely to get on with, who will put you at ease, and whom he thinks you probably should avoid. Don't forget you know each other well, so he is likely to know the kind of people that you respond well to and steer you towards them. In a corporate environment, this can make the event seem a little less daunting.

In the early days, I was nervous walking into the corporate events. My head would be spinning with etiquette – how would I come across? Would I be able to make conversation? Would I be stuck with the boring person, or would they find me boring? Then I coaxed myself into thinking that each event was an opportunity to have a pleasant time, and I deliberately use the word "pleasant". I did not aim for a "good" or "great" time as I didn't want to give myself the extra pressure of high expectations. It was a chance to meet people, most of whom would hopefully be interesting. If we didn't hit the spot socially, I would still learn from the experience, and could grow with the discovery of what I liked in other people. Even if the event itself didn't go well, I still had my marriage, my family, my children, and my social network.

The very first time I ever accompanied Andrew to a corporate event, it was in the early days when he was starting to establish himself and his reputation within his profession. He was becoming a known name in the industry and was on the verge of being recognised as an expert in his field. So the corporate entertaining events really mattered. The need for them to be successful had ramped up a few notches.

I knew Andrew was eagerly anticipating the event as he wanted to nurture many business relationships with the people who were going to be in attendance. As it was my very first time accompanying him to a corporate event, I automatically assumed I would be expected to be physically by his side all evening – the dynamic, smiling, united husband and wife. So you can imagine my horror when I was distracted for a moment, and when I turned back, I couldn't see Andrew anywhere. We had literally just arrived and I couldn't even spot him in the crowd.

So before panic set in, how did I react?

I made a beeline for one of my husband's colleagues, whom I already knew well. He was with his wife, talking with a couple of clients and their wives.

Waiting for a pause in conversation, I smiled and said, "Do you mind if I join you?"

I would discourage you from saying something along the lines of, "Can I gate-crash your group?" as this gives a very different first impression. You are basically seeking approval for the action you have clearly just carried out, so it's not the best way to start a conversation.

If someone asks, "Do you mind if I join you?" there is rarely a time when anyone would reply with, "Yes, we do. Go away!" People tend to welcome others who are prepared to make an effort, and that includes at a corporate event.

So what did I say next?

"I'm married to Andrew Watson. My name is Sarah. We've just arrived, but I've lost him already, so I thought I would come over and introduce myself."

And so a conversation had started. Phew!

Note that I did not make any negative comment about losing my husband. If I had burst into the group, panic-stricken at being left alone already, any sympathy would probably have been directed towards my husband rather than me. Instead, I acknowledged that I'd arrived with him to the group as he was the reason I was actually at the event, so it helped to explain who I was. My straightforward explanation, in turn, gave those people the opportunity to approach my husband and say they had just met me, thereby creating a potential starting point for their own conversation.

Over the years, it has varied as to whether Andrew and I stay in each other's company at corporate events or effectively go our separate ways. The time we spend together varies depending on the type of event and other guests in attendance. Andrew has always been relaxed about whether I stay with him or socialise independently, but some professionals dread corporate entertaining, preferring their wives to remain by their side for comfort and support.

Asking your husband before the event takes place and understanding what he expects from you will play to your advantage.

# First Contact

Looking people in the eye is crucial. A proper handshake is crucial. Smiling is crucial. Acknowledging the person verbally is crucial.

All this is simple courtesy and common sense. If you greet a person with warmth and a friendly demeanour, the interaction gets off to a good start. They will gain an impression of you in those first few moments, so make sure it's the right one as you only get one chance.

When I was meeting people at corporate events for the first time, or even if I had met them before but still didn't know them very well, I had two main thought processes with my approach. I reminded myself that the person I wanted to talk to could be shyer than me and nervous about making an effort, so I persuaded myself that my bravery was doing us both a favour! I still take that approach.

I also remembered that most people enjoy talking about themselves, even shy people. Therefore I would ask questions that showed my interest in the people I was meeting within the corporate environment. If you show an interest in people, it is a great way of breaking the ice, and they usually make a comment that you can build on to develop the conversation later on.

If the person I was talking to asked about me in return, I would respond with a simple answer rather than dominating the conversation. If they wanted to know more, they would ask. Give enough of a response to engage in conversation, but hold back initially to enable different conversations to flow later on. Rest assured – this approach was not based on me being nervous or unsure of the person I was talking to, or even that I was trying to create an air of mystery about myself. My view was that if I told the whole story, chapter and verse, what would the listener be left with? If I've said it all, all they can do is acknowledge what I've just said. End of that particular line of conversation.

This was a dilemma I was faced with as I was building up my understanding of the corporate networking environment. Now, being in that environment feels natural and automatic, and I obviously hope this will become the case for you too.

Let's give an example to demonstrate what I mean about showing an interest in others.

I am meeting a client and his wife for the first time at an event. The wife and I have swapped pleasantries, and we now need to get a conversation flowing.

She then says, "Today was a bit chaotic before coming here as my daughter is teething and was having a bad day."

I could respond in one of two ways.

"My children had a terrible time with teething too – let me tell you how I dealt with it…"

I have instantly shut her off, preferring to give her my apparent expertise rather than listening to her, thereby closing down any flow of conversation.

Instead I could respond by saying, "That's a shame – how old is she?" or "I can't recall how long children are teething for. Do you think it will improve soon?" or "Do you have other children? Did they have problems with teething too?"

I'm sure you can see the difference. The second approach responds to her comment in the correct way. I am showing that I am listening, I am not shutting her down to get my own view across, and I am keeping the flow of conversation going.

The person you are talking to may have talked about their day, and the challenges they had in relation to workload or travel arrangements.

They might ask a question such as, "Did you have to juggle work commitments today in order to be here?"

If you answer, "No" it naturally closes that topic of conversation. It would be better to say, "I was fortunate that today is not a working day for me. I do voluntary work on a Thursday (for example) so was lucky that I didn't have to juggle too many other tasks to get here on time."

That informs the other person that you work, but not every day. They now know you do voluntary work, but you haven't said what. This gives them the opportunity to pursue either of those points if the conversation shows signs of drying up, thereby helping to continue it. If you give just enough information without the detailed explanation, then the listener can make some remark based on their own experience by way of comparison, and a better level of conversation will flow. That theory works the other way around too, so it is crucial to pay attention to what the other person is telling you as you can build on it later.

Don't feel too disheartened if the topic of conversation does not appeal to you. In the networking environment, everyone in attendance – including the Corporate Wife – needs to engage in conversation regardless of whether they find it stimulating or not. When I reflect on this aspect of corporate events, I recall the "small talk" topics happen in the early stages of the event. As people relax and settle into the atmosphere, a more interesting range of topics will surface.

## Comfort Zone

People love their comfort zone. It's reassuring, safe, easy and relaxed. Equally, they find themselves taken out of their comfort zone at regular times during their lives.

People prosper and learn from the world around them and their own reaction to it.

If you really dread the thought of the corporate networking environment, I want to persuade you to step out of your comfort zone and give it a try.

Everyone who is making an effort in their corporate networking environment is doing so to make their career and professional path a success. They need the support of others for their own endeavours and achievements. Ultimately your professional partner will succeed based upon his professional ability, but corporate networking provides an environment to reinforce the character that other professionals are dealing with. So much time is spent in the workplace and people will find that time easier if they can make a connection with the people they are working alongside. Attending the networking events with your husband is your way of making the simple statement that you support him, his efforts and ambition to succeed, and you are willing and happy to give your own personal time to prove it.

Being taken out of your comfort zone has huge rewards. As the introduction to this book stated, a friend noticed that I had "worked the room" at a corporate event. At some point, and I'm not even sure when that point came, I took myself out of my comfort zone, showing my support for Andrew by joining him in his networking environment.

Is the corporate networking environment so different to other aspects of your life? There will have been plenty of situations that have taken you out of your comfort zone. The role of a Corporate Wife is another example, the only difference being that you are taking on that role for a specific reason which is not about you specifically. Stepping out of your comfort zone and into the corporate networking environment as a Corporate Wife, you are not acting for your own gain, but for the gain of your partner. It is a unique task, which is why some might describe it as a skill.

When I reflect on my role as a Corporate Wife, I realise that I have carried out that duty without question or analysis. I stepped out of my comfort zone a long time ago, and now see being a Corporate Wife as another part of my day-to-day life. My duty as a Corporate Wife has – for some time now – been just as much in my comfort zone as anything else that I do.

If the prospect of carrying out the role of the Corporate Wife still fills you with dread, consider that the other spouses and partners in the room will be in the same position as you. They will also have stepped out of their comfort zones to make the effort for their loved ones, so you are in the same situation, with the same thought processes, apprehensions and hopes that you will find the corporate event an enjoyable success.

Conversations at corporate events can vary depending on whether the attendees wish to discuss business or pleasure. The time obviously passes more pleasantly for the spouses and partners if those present wish to talk pleasure, i.e. show a general interest in each other. But if you are attending an event where the business talk dominates the conversation, so be it. If business talk all evening takes you out of your comfort zone, don't worry too much. Business is after all the starting point and the reason why you all came together in the first place. The corporate etiquette is that you show an interest in the subject rather than changing the topic to one that is of particular interest to you.

# Being A Corporate Guest

There are different starting points when attending an event as a corporate guest. The hosting professional may wish to develop a new or existing business relationship with your husband, or they may be hosting the event as a thank you for your husband's assistance with a recent business transaction or connection. Alternatively, it may be to acknowledge the ongoing importance of your husband to the host in a business capacity.

When you are invited to a corporate event, your husband will carry out the courtesy of responding to the invitation and thanking the host afterwards. By all means express gratitude at the invitation in person, as manners are always correct, but do not feel obliged to hold court or entertain everyone. Be mindful of your role of support, especially when you are a guest.

When you're attending an event such as a dinner or theatre performance, the format for the event tends to be almost predictable. However, whilst the format for certain corporate events will be straightforward, there are others that will engage the guests in different ways. For many years, Andrew co-hosted an afternoon at the Chelsea Flower Show. The guest list altered slightly each year – clients and their spouses/partners were invited, and Andrew's colleagues and spouses/partners would also be in attendance.

The afternoon would start with lunch in a stunning London restaurant, after which we would make our way to the Chelsea Flower Show. Whilst Andrew hosted this particular event over successive years, the style of the day varied greatly. One year the majority of clients and their partners wanted to wander around the show by themselves. Another year, we broke off into smaller groups to stroll around together. There was a year when we didn't get away from the Champagne Tent!

When you're attending an event such as the Chelsea Flower Show, there are no "rules" for how the day will progress. Despite the fact that year after year different clients responded differently to the invitation, each event was deemed a great success by all involved.

Whether you are attending an event as a host or a guest, you may find other guests are slightly "frazzled" and offload their woes about their bad day or how problematic getting to the event was for them. If you've had a bad journey or dealt with various home stresses before you arrived at the venue, I'd advise you not to share them with other people. Even if you then settle down and are utterly charming for the remainder of the event, they will remember your negative behaviour in those first few moments.

If your husband is hosting, allow your guests the opportunity to moan about their circumstances if they want to, but the Corporate Wife must appear calm, relaxed and in control of most situations. By all means show them sympathy (even if you do not feel especially sympathetic) as they will then think positively towards you. It may in fact be nerves causing them to vent, so being polite and supportive, you will help to defuse any personal tension they might be feeling.

Think again about the reason you are in attendance at the corporate event. In your capacity as a Corporate Wife, you are there for a purpose – to support your professional partner. The purpose of the event is to acknowledge business connections, so it is not a situation where you vent any frustrations. The proper corporate etiquette is to keep your own counsel and graciously take on the supportive role. You will no doubt have plenty of close family and friends to whom you can vent any general frustrations, so please do not offload your woes within the corporate environment. If you do, ultimately your husband will be remembered as attending the event with "the wife who was moaning".

As well as those who voice their woes, I have also witnessed spouses using the event as an opportunity to snipe on behalf of their husbands. Professional life is demanding, and sometimes the work environment doesn't run smoothly. Even if your husband is arguing with every member of his team, is under tremendous pressure in his work environment, is losing sleep due to the anxiety of it all, if you find yourself standing alongside his colleagues, say nothing. You can be his confidante at home, but the corporate environment is not the place for you to fight his corner. Regardless of whatever pressure he is under, it is ultimately *his* working environment, so you must remain cool, calm and corporate at all times.

# Being A Corporate Host

If your husband is hosting (or co-hosting) an event, it is of the utmost importance that you arrive in good time *before* the guests. Allow time to compose yourself and make yourself aware of any relevant information about the attending guests or running programme for the evening. This is probably the most important scenario for the Corporate Wife. If your husband is established enough within his field to be co-hosting or hosting an event, stand alongside him.

When your husband is hosting an event, you need to "work the room", demonstrating support, enthusiasm and interest. Be approachable. It is a time when you really are "on show", and you have to get it right.

This is quite a task, but it isn't as scary, or as difficult, as it sounds. Remind yourself of when you have family or friends over to your home – you talk to each of them, catch up with their news and see how they are. It's a similar scenario when hosting corporate events, the main difference being that in the corporate environment you are not hosting friends and family, but people who matter to your husband in relation to his business life. You will not know many of them, their personalities, their lifestyles, hobbies, interests, etc., but as the wife of the host, it's your duty to show an interest in each of them before they put their coats back on to head home.

Let's take that a step further. If you are in conversation with a client whom your husband has had regular dealings with, touch on that point when speaking to them, acknowledging their importance to your husband. This can only be flattering to the client concerned. Equally, if the client is someone your husband wishes to develop a business relationship with, show an interest in that person to aid your husband's efforts.

Whilst it is important to acknowledge your husband's clients, it is just as important to acknowledge their partners. If I focused on talking to the client and ignored his wife, how would she perceive me? It would without doubt affect her opinion of me. She would voice her observation to her husband (hopefully in private), and he would then develop a perception of me based on what she'd told him.

The client's wife – like everyone else – may be feeling a little out of her comfort zone at the corporate event. She may be feeling anxious, thinking the event won't be that enjoyable, or she may really dislike corporate entertaining. Then the host's wife walks in, looking confident, and chats easily to her husband while ignoring her. Even if the client's wife is reluctant to embrace the evening, if your husband is hosting, you have to step up and make the first move to interact with her, and as many other people as possible.

If the event is large on guest numbers, of course it is impossible to interact with everyone. If that is the case, ask your husband well in advance who the important guests to him will be, and those are the people you focus on.

When your husband is hosting a smaller scale corporate event, such as a dinner, it is generally to acknowledge a more personal business connection. Events such as a dinner are by their nature more personal, and tend to occur when your husband and the client have developed a long-standing business relationship and mutual respect for each other's professional ability. It is important, however, to remind yourself that it is a business event, and you have a role to fulfil. Even if your husband appears relaxed and not in "work mode", your behaviour will still reflect on him and be remembered by the other people present.

Imagine joining your husband for dinner with a client and his wife. Your husband and the client have just completed a lucrative deal, which has boosted the client's status within his firm, and your husband fronted his own team pitching for the job. His long-standing business relationship with the client no doubt helped to cement the deal, and as a thank you, he has invited the client and his wife to dinner.

At pre-dinner drinks, the client's wife openly states that she will order the most expensive cocktails on the menu. She consumes the drinks at a tremendous rate, frantically clicking her fingers at the waiter to be "restocked", much to her own amusement. Then, when you all sit down for dinner, she ostentatiously orders the most expensive dish.

There is a school of thought that would say her husband is the client, so she has every right to order whatever she wants. But looking at the mutual importance of the business relationship, don't you think her behaviour would cause her husband embarrassment? Your husband, being the professional he is, would probably neither refuse nor comment on her demands, but naturally he will notice the open nature of her readiness to spend his (or his firm's) money.

Whatever the nature of the business relationship, whatever the reason behind coming together in a corporate capacity, it is important to understand and acknowledge the rules of corporate etiquette. Even if a corporate event is covered on business expenses, you do not abuse the hospitality.

Let's imagine another scenario. The host is very nervous about the success of his event. He has spent a lot of time planning the guest list, agreeing the menu, and arranging the seating plan. Whilst he's greeting his guests, you notice he keeps looking at the front door of the venue.

His wife is late.

When she arrives, she looks rather harassed and stands in the background, talking to a member of the venue staff. She takes a huge gulp of her drink, spilling it onto her dress, then turns her back on the group whilst dabbing at it with a tissue. Her husband's eyes dart back and forth – he is in charge of the event, and has the task of greeting and meeting everyone in attendance, including the corporate guests' partners, but he's having to do this without his wife by his side. How many guests do you think would notice? Most of them, probably.

If your husband is the host, then you are too.

# Conversation Starters

Many would agree that the task of starting a conversation is the most difficult part of corporate entertaining and etiquette. You have stepped out of your familiar day-to-day life into a situation where you probably don't know many people, then you are expected to start friendly, engaging conversations. Oh, deep joy.

Much as you might like to, you can't spend the entire event sitting in a chair in the corner, people watching. You can't go to the other extreme either, allowing your nerves to create a noisy hyper version of your usual charming self. So how do you find the middle ground where you interact with others whilst remaining aware of corporate etiquette and the role of supporting your partner?

Before you run for the hills, here are some ideas for conversation starters when you're meeting people for the first time.

"Pleasure to meet you…"

Note the deliberate use of the word "Pleasure" – if you are meeting someone for the first time, it demonstrates manners and an acceptable level of warmth. I tend not to use phrases like "It's so nice to meet you!" or "How lovely to meet you!" when I am meeting people for the first time in a corporate environment. Remember you are there for the purpose of supporting your partner, not to make friends. Be charming and carry out the Corporate Wife role.

You may discover that the person you are meeting for the first time is especially nice. Alternatively, they may be especially unpleasant. Or you may never find out at all, as you are meeting them at an event specifically for corporate networking. Making initial contact with too much warmth and compassion may leave you feeling a little lost if they do not return the same level of friendliness.

If I know that the client I'm addressing is important to my husband, I use one of the following opening sentences: "It's nice to meet you – Andrew has mentioned you to me," or "It's lovely to finally meet you."

These are complimentary remarks aimed at that person specifically – it lets them know that Andrew feels they are worth talking about, and demonstrates respect for their business connection.

If your husband and the client have a strong working connection, show more warmth with your choice of words, as this demonstrates your understanding of how important they are to your husband.

So you've got off the starting block by acknowledging the person, but what next?

"Did you have to travel far to get here?"

Not very inspiring, I know, but it covers a few minutes whilst they explain their journey. If they had a difficult journey, that's a genuine shame, but it's great from the point of view of starting a conversation. Their story will cover a few more minutes whilst you warm up.

Listen out for passing remarks, as they can be useful when developing more conversation. For example, the person you are talking to may say, "I thought I might miss the train, as the traffic was bad when I dropped the children off."

That can trigger a whole host of questions: what are the children's ages?

Who looks after them? Do family live nearby? Etc.

Another topic could be: "Isn't this a beautiful venue?" They will no doubt agree (they recognise corporate etiquette too, after all), and may offer further comment. For example, they may have visited the venue before or know something about the history of the location, so you can build a conversation on that topic.

If that line of conversation dries up, you can ask whether they have attended similar venues for other corporate events. If they have, you can ask where they were and whether they have a preference for a particular type of event, building the conversation from that angle instead.

Not working for you? How about asking how much corporate entertaining they get involved with; whether attending corporate events means they have to juggle other aspects of their life; whether they know any other people in attendance; whether they socialise with their husband's colleagues and wives.

I'm not suggesting for a moment that you rattle off question after question; these are just some ideas to help get a conversation started. It doesn't have to be an intriguing topic, just a general starting block conversation to put everyone at ease and develop rapport.

You may also find that another person attending the event will see you talking and will come and join you. They can then add to the conversation. Don't forget, lots of people find the task of conversation starting a challenge, so for some it's less daunting to join an established conversation.

The key to successfully carrying out your Corporate Wife role at events is to talk just enough, then listen. Any conversation can build from a passing remark. Ask open questions – What? Why? How? If you ask a closed question, the person you are talking to may not be able to continue with any flow of conversation. Remember, they may well be far more anxious than you and will probably not care what the topic of your conversation is. They will just be grateful to be talking about something.

# Conversation Stoppers

Now and then, someone behaves in such a way or makes a remark that stops the interaction in its tracks. The good news is that in your capacity as Corporate Wife, it isn't necessarily your task to rescue the situation, but it is corporate etiquette not to react or respond if something negative happens around you. If something goes wrong, it is not your role to intervene or voice an opinion.

Conversation stoppers are not a common occurrence, but they can and do happen. The main skill for the Corporate Wife is to react with dignity and restraint.

So what do I regard as a conversation stopper? Whilst everyone would have a slightly different view, it tends to be an offensive remark, disrespectful behaviour, or a strong opinion that is socially challenging.

People aren't generally offensive as their default setting. At a corporate event, alcohol could be a contributing factor, or possibly something outside the corporate networking scene is affecting a person's behaviour at that particular moment. Regardless of how angry or offended you feel by their remark, do not react. It is likely that the person making the offensive remark will be taken aback by their own behaviour, so if you react negatively too, the remark turns into an interaction.

If you are really offended by someone's behaviour or remark, make polite excuses and move away from the person concerned. Your husband will no doubt be aware of the type of remarks that will cause you offence, and will be grateful that you did not react and escalate the situation in his networking environment.

It's the same if someone demonstrates disrespectful behaviour. I suspect there have been times when you have experienced someone behaving negatively, but I doubt you immediately stepped in. Similar rules apply within the corporate environment. You are welcome to air your opinion to your husband within the comfort of your own home, but in the corporate environment, look at the bigger picture – leave the role of the offender to the offender. You don't want to end up being the topic of conversation because you reacted or voiced your own view. No matter how frustrating or offensive the situation is, don't react.

If someone voices a strong opinion that is socially challenging, so be it. Feel sympathy for them. Just because they say something that you do not agree with on any level, it doesn't make the corporate environment the place for you, as a Corporate Wife, to challenge their view. You may in fact learn from their different viewpoint either challenging your thoughts or confirming your personal beliefs.

We recognise our own values from watching and listening to others, so see a conversation stopper as an opportunity to clarify our own thoughts. Even if the conversation stopper tries to draw you in and challenge you, my strong advice is that you keep quiet, no matter how difficult a challenge that may be. Keep your own counsel, and you will be conducting yourself with the correct level of corporate etiquette.

# Outsider Information

Never underestimate the benefits to your husband of you attending events in his networking environment. You can provide him with an "outsider" view on his business contacts. Don't forget – in your role as a Corporate Wife, you do not have a business relationship with the people you are meeting, so they may drop their guard in front of you.

I share my observations with my husband after the event. Whilst I realise others might not do this, I would suggest that any observations you make are helpful for your husband. They create a broader picture of the people he is interacting with in his professional career, and can give him more understanding of different professional situations. By passing on your observations, you are giving him another person's perspective, which will help him when he's considering the dynamic of the business relationship.

To put that into context, let's say you are attending an event and listening to an assistant from a client's firm. You know this firm is important to your husband's professional progression and success. The assistant makes a subtle negative remark about his boss, or you notice that he rolls his eyes when the boss speaks – that *could* suggest there is friction amongst the client's team. The assistant could even be considering moving on to a new job. Any observation you can relay to your husband will help him complete the bigger picture.

Let's say your hunch is right. You've noticed the negative remark or the rolling of the eyes, and that information gives your husband the opportunity to consider the client firm's internal relationships and how they could have a knock-on effect for him. So we consider the assistant's behaviour first. If your husband values the working relationship with the assistant, he will want that to continue, regardless of whether the assistant stays where he is or moves on. If the assistant stays put, the relationship can continue. If he moves on, your husband will need to invest time building relationships with that assistant's new colleagues.

Now let's consider the options from the boss's point of view. He may be near retirement, and the team might feel he is currently holding them back. He may wish to continue in his role for the foreseeable future, but recognises that the assistant is a negative influence on the team. He may be watching the assistant, considering whether to continue that particular working relationship. If the boss and assistant part company, there will be a vacancy within the client's team. When it's filled, your husband will need to make contact with the new assistant and develop a business connection with him or her.

If you have decided not to pass any comment on your observation to your husband, there might come a day when he comes home and says that he has lost a major client or contract because the client team has parted company. It happens. If only your husband had been aware of your observations, he would have had a bigger picture with which to maintain strong professional relationships, regardless of whether the client team stayed together or went their separate ways.

I'm not for a minute suggesting that Andrew and I sit down formally and talk through an event and its attendees. I am merely putting it to you that any observation you pass on can be of use to your partner, regardless of how small the observation may be. There have been so many useful pieces of information I have passed on over the years as a Corporate Wife. People have expressed excitement at new business projects, disappointment with ventures, mentioned positive and negative experiences of other professionals in the industry, etc. Every piece of information is useful to a professional when they are investing so much time and energy into their success.

The same applies to personal information that you learn of whilst in the corporate networking environment. You may hear about promotions (for the client or their spouse), personal celebrations, milestones, weddings, anniversaries, funerals – just about anything! If you pass that information on, your husband will have the opportunity to acknowledge the event to the client (whether it is good or bad) when he next makes contact with them, which will demonstrate his interest in the client. The personal information the client has chosen to disclose therefore increases the positive connection in their working relationship with your husband.

# Dos and Don'ts

**Do** try to enjoy corporate entertaining – it is likely you will be spending time in an environment or at an event that you wouldn't otherwise get to experience, so make the most of it.

**Do** show warmth, and demonstrate a confident, friendly demeanour. It will go a long way to making sure you're remembered in a positive light, which will have a knock-on effect for your husband too.

**Do** ask people about themselves – everyone has a story, and everyone likes to talk about themselves. If you show an interest in them, they are more likely to return the compliment.

**Do** communicate with your husband before the event, if you feel it would help you. Find out the people attending the event who matter to him, whom he wishes to develop contact with, whom he wishes to avoid. Any information is useful so you can support your husband based on background knowledge.

If the event has a large guest list, you don't want to waste time in conversation with someone who does not click with your husband in the business environment. Instead, **do** spend time with those who are important, supportive and approachable.

**Do** inform your husband of your observations, and of any comments made, which you think will assist his professional engagement. These can be anything from the dynamics within a client's team to a wife discussing a forthcoming personal event such as an anniversary or birthday. If your husband has that information fed back to him, he can potentially win the client's confidence by acknowledging a personal celebration.

**Do** allow yourself time to get to the event, making sure your home arrangements are in place so you can relax once you are in attendance. Make the time to visit the "Ladies" before you arrive, so you don't feel uncomfortable or distracted. Do also consider the "just in case" contents in your handbag.

**Don't** make the assumption that their career is just a small part of the professional's life. In a lot of cases, it dominates their life. Professionals want to achieve and succeed. They put pressure on themselves, which at times can feel relentless.

**Don't** forget that the purpose of the event is business networking. You are there to support your partner, so please do not hold court or feel frustrated that people are not showing enough interest in you. It is *his* working environment.

**Don't** drink excessively, even if the majority of people in attendance are doing so. You will have plenty of opportunities in your private life to let your hair down, but the corporate environment is not one of them. Equally, do not show any reaction to somebody who has drunk too much. You don't want them to remember you in their hangover haze as one of the people staring at them in disgust.

**Don't** challenge anyone on his or her personal views and opinions, even if it is a topic you feel strongly about. Exercise diplomacy. Others may share your views, but stand back and let them engage in a showdown if they feel it's necessary. When on duty as a Corporate Wife, you are not there to convert others to your point of view.

That said, please **don't** stand quietly and not speak at all. It is very difficult for people to engage with someone who does not give anything in return, which makes the situation difficult for all concerned. You'll give a bad first impression, regardless of the real you. Have something to contribute without taking over.

**Don't** forget to smile!

# Understanding Different Characters

You will definitely meet some colourful characters in your capacity as a Corporate Wife. Some may not be the kind of people that your husband is happy to engage with, but he won't have a choice in the matter – he *has* to interact with them as part of his continued progression and success in the workplace.

I have listed below some different character traits with suggestions on how to deal with them.

**The Climber:** These people are very driven, almost to the point of trying so hard to make an impact that they lose the ability to register anything going on around them. They dominate conversations and are not good at listening – listening is of no interest to them. Their purpose is to create a strong image, but usually without the expertise to back it up.

The Climber will keep their phone with them at all times, and check it regularly (even when in the company of others). They tend to talk a good game, but in a professional capacity they get held back for not being a team player so rise through the ranks at a slower rate than their peers. However, they are usually too caught up on their own image to notice.

The main method of interaction with the Climbers is to keep quiet and listen, as that's all they require of you.

**The Weakest Link:** These are the people who are always present, but rarely noticed. They don't have a client base, don't have any presence at events, and even seem to be off the radar within their own team. The Weakest Link is happy to stand back and watch others interact, and it takes a lot of effort to engage them in conversation. Even if you're successful, you'll normally only open a short-term platform for them to express dull views on random subjects that the receiver cannot go anywhere with.

The Weakest Link requires a smile, a nod, a few kind passing remarks, then they are happy to go back to their favourite stance of "blending in".

**The 5 Minute Rule:** This type gives 5 minutes more than everyone else. They have to be the last to leave, regardless of the hour or success of the event. This is not generally based on insecurity, but intrigue. What could happen if they put in a little more effort than those who have just left? What could 5 more minutes of networking bring them?

You cannot deter the 5 Minute Rule – simply say your goodbyes and leave the venue. They will follow on 5 minutes later, content there is nothing more to be done. For the time being.

**The Snake:** A dangerous breed, and definitely one to recognise quickly. The Snake tends to snipe at or criticise others when in company, trying to catch you off guard so they feel victorious (or that they have you as an ally). They never actually voice their opinion to the person it concerns, though. Some would say their behaviour is deflective as they doubt their own professional success, but they can be damaging.

Do not give anything away to Snakes. Keep the conversation neutral, but be ready to bite back in the most diplomatic way possible when they go on the attack. You will then not appear confrontational, but you'll give the Snake the message you won't be messed with.

**The Bored:** They've had enough of their job, their commute, paying the bills, their most recent holiday destination – everything. Getting a smile from them is near on impossible, let alone an interesting exchange of views and opinion. The only way to deal with the Bored is to let them whine – they won't realise they are whining, as they are too caught up in how dreadful life is.

The best outcome from an interaction with the Bored is that you feel more positive about your own life, and are relieved to learn you are not as negative as some others. My suggestion is to put the ball in their court by asking them what they are interested in, and what topics they enjoy discussing – but it is not your job to coax them into positive conversation if they are determined to squash all efforts.

**The Creep:** He communicates with your cleavage instead of your face, taking every opportunity to make a raunchy remark, usually followed by a bellowing laugh whilst turning his head to each member of his audience for agreement. He isn't bothered by business chat, instead wanting fine wine and lots of ladies to stare at.

Just pretend he is funny to prevent the situation becoming awkward, and accept that as the night goes on, he will physically lean on you as he becomes more intoxicated and tired. Then he will suddenly disappear to find his way home to his bed. The following day he will head into work, claiming to be free from hangover and relaying to anyone who will listen that he had another "jolly good night".

**The Charmer:** He will be on call, to hand and responsive all night, demonstrating gentlemanly qualities from the start, holding eye contact with you when you speak, acknowledging and agreeing with every comment you make. He will take your coat without being prompted, way before it crosses your husband's mind to offer the same gesture; he will replenish your drink regularly, check you are enjoying your evening, and show an almost abnormal interest in you and your life.

You will likely have an aching face by the end of an evening in the company of the Charmer, as your fixed grin will be stuck for hours as you graciously acknowledge the high level of attention. The intensity will be exhausting, but the Charmer will leave the event happy in the knowledge that he has treated another lady like a lady.

**The Closed Book:** The Closed Book has similar traits to the Bored. Even though you are attending a corporate event, he openly states that he does not want to discuss work, that he is "off duty". He leaves you hanging whilst you frantically try to resurrect your small talk options, shutting down most topics of conversation with an air of superiority.

If you are on your own with the Closed Book, it is easier to count your losses, warmly state that it was a pleasure to meet him, and move on – he believes he is worldly wise and above the pointless activity of small talk. If you are within a group, you can then converse with someone else who may have witnessed your efforts with the Closed Book and be silently sympathising with you.

**The Money Chasers:** When Andrew and I got engaged, I recall one lady telling me I was "sorted". Another asked whether I would resign from my job before or after the wedding. Sadly, you will always find people who are attracted to the money and not the person, but I'm glad to say I haven't come across many people who are like this.

When I was a PA, I saw others who had no shame in getting up to mischief. I knew there was a risk of me being stereotyped as Andrew and I met at work, but I was relaxed enough to think that if it didn't work out between us, then so be it. I would simply carry on with my life. More than 20 years later, we are still together.

No doubt there are Money Chasers out there, but I hope professionals have the sense to recognise them and not be suckered in.

**The Drunk:** Every event has the Drunk in attendance. He goes too far, slurs his words, doesn't form clear sentences and barges past people to get to the bar. He will sometimes lose the ability to finish the contents of his own glass before replenishing his neighbour's glass, insisting that everyone nearby joins him for "just one more" regardless of protests or polite refusals. If persuaded to leave, the Drunk staggers away, no doubt muttering about the event finishing early, or everyone "being boring" because they're heading home.

The easiest option is to agree with most of what the Drunk says to lessen the risk of him becoming moody through the drunken haze. No one will be able to contact him the following day. His PA will cover for him with the excuse of a short notice meeting whilst he sleeps it off at home – or on his office meeting room floor if he upset the Wife.

# Survival Skills

Whilst it is easy to focus on some of the challenging aspects of being a Corporate Wife, if you recognise the importance of your own role, then you can provide an active contribution to making the professional commitment work. It is an honourable gesture to offer a loved one your support based purely on their gain and not yours. Standing beside your partner, you confirm your understanding of the commitment, determination, drive and ambition that he must demonstrate in order to succeed in his chosen field, indicating the belief you have in him.

Whilst raising our two boys, I have had an enjoyable social life with and without my husband. I have managed various voluntary roles over the years, and have had, and am currently in, paid work.

The role of a Corporate Wife will become part of your existing life, carried out along with everything else you do, and whilst at times it can be demanding, it does not come at the cost of other aspects of your life.

What you get out of your life depends on what *you* put in. It is not defined by others. Don't look to your professional husband to define who you are, but use the time that he is away from home, building his professional reputation, to develop and define yourself. Having your own identity is important (to you both).

There are different aspects to every person – different views, passions, hobbies, characteristics – which no one should lose sight of. They are the traits that attracted your husband to you in the first place, so have the confidence to feel comfortable knowing who you are, and be true to yourself. However, regardless of your views, passions, hobbies and characteristics, your role as a Corporate Wife means you need to set aside those traits when you're in the networking environment. Simply attend to demonstrate your support for your husband.

In your capacity as a Corporate Wife, you fulfil an important role which will enrich your experience of life and benefit your husband in his quest to create a successful professional career. He will come together with other professionals based on their connection through work, aware that he has to make that commitment to the networking environment in order to progress and succeed. That duty will be easier for him to honour with you standing alongside him.

If you meet people within the corporate environment whom you do not connect with, your own life will remain the same despite the experience of the networking event. You have the advantage as you are supporting your husband without any pressure on you personally to establish long-term connections with those you meet in his network.

When I look back on my role as a Corporate Wife, I reflect on the many pleasant and entertaining experiences that it has created for me. I have been to beautiful venues, met a huge variety of people, and learnt so much from each experience. I have also witnessed some people who felt they had to make a point, or challenge the environment they were in, which showed their lack of respect for the importance of corporate etiquette. Too many times, I have watched people air opinions which were simply unnecessary or inappropriate within the corporate environment. I have watched interactions between people, and found them almost confusing. Why didn't they feel able to behave with corporate etiquette? What did they gain?

If you act within the boundaries of corporate etiquette, you are no less a person. Your views do not diminish, or lose their value. You are simply responding to that environment in a way that is needed, and that shows your respect for the network. It isn't, generally speaking, a natural environment for anyone; the professionals feel pressure to achieve and impress, and some Corporate Wives can struggle with understanding their place in that environment, but still at times I am surprised that some wives do not grasp the importance of showing their support. Please don't think for a moment that I am saying the majority of people get it wrong as most get it right, but not everyone shares the same approach, or understands what needs to be done.

Nonetheless, I find people fascinating. They have an incredible range of opinions, reactions and behaviour patterns. Throughout my time at work, and not just in my capacity as a Corporate Wife, I have seen a huge range of interactions within a business setting. I have witnessed junior members of staff blushing and flirting with more senior employees. I have seen colleagues burst into tears through their fear of making a bad impression with clients. I have watched assistants try to belittle their bosses publicly through so-called humour.

Every occasion, good and bad, has an impact in some way on the corporate environment. We are all responsible for the smooth running of the business environment, whether we touch on it through our own work or within the role of a Corporate Wife.

I was once attending my firm's Christmas party. There was a buffet supper, and no fixed seating plan. The Managing Partner was an older gentleman, who looked tired and a little out of place. He had a plate of food and was looking around for somewhere to sit.

I was sitting with other secretaries, and we shuffled along the bench, inviting him to take a seat. We spoke for a while, making small talk – I recall we chatted about a holiday that he had recently taken with his wife – but being at that party clearly wasn't his natural environment, and I felt sympathetic towards him. After the brief encounter, he moved on and our evening continued.

Now the fascinating part of this story is that minutes later, one of my bosses appeared.

"What did you say to him?" he barked. "What on earth were you doing, talking to him?"

I relayed our conversation, and explained that the Managing Partner had been holding a plate of food, but had nowhere to sit.

My boss then asked, "Do you realise who he is?" to which I replied that I did. My boss wanted to know if I had told the Managing Partner whom I worked for. I replied that I had not, pointing out that when the Managing Partner reflected on his evening, he would no doubt remember myself and the other secretaries for making the effort to talk to him, but he would not recall any interaction with my boss.

So what is the message in that story? Different people approach situations in different ways. I did not see the Managing Partner as someone to be in awe of, but rather that he was out of his comfort zone and looking tired. Nonetheless, he was still there, in attendance, doing what he had to do.

Think of the bigger picture, and what you can do to help. Your survival in the role of Corporate Wife depends on your approach. If you wish to be the person who stands back, you will not gain any benefit or enjoyment from the environment you are in. If you take the plunge and embrace the situation, you are more likely to gain something positive from the experience. I personally find it intriguing and exciting to observe and be around other people – those first few minutes create impressions, helping to develop our ability to interact with people we don't know, which in turn develops our confidence. The interaction also helps to clarify our own likes and dislikes, and our observation of how others come across convinces us whether we want to mirror them or act in contrast.

# In Summary

Everyone is aware of etiquette. There are different rules of etiquette within the corporate environment which I have demonstrated in this handbook.

It is perfectly acceptable to respect the corporate environment, and your involvement in the corporate world can enrich your life, rather than have a negative impact upon it. It is a valued and important job to support your husband with his corporate career. Whilst it dominates his life, it does not dominate yours, and you are still free to live your life as you wish – within the mutual commitment of your relationship, of course.

The networking environment exists to cement business relationships or create new ones. It does not take place for purely social reasons. You are there, in your capacity as a Corporate Wife, to support the success of the business connection, and to demonstrate your understanding of the hopes and ambitions of your partner. If you understand the commitment your husband has to give, the long hours, the challenges and goals, then your support will make that journey more bearable for him.

Be proud that you can usefully be part of your husband's working environment. Be proud to support him in the challenging and fast-moving world he has chosen to make his mark in. Supporting a professional is invaluable. You will attend the corporate events because he wants you there; he wants you to interact with his colleagues and clients; he wants you to complete the picture of him for his business contacts.

Step out of your comfort zone. It's worth it for the feeling of satisfaction, knowing you are doing right by your partner whilst enjoying an interesting and fascinating journey along the way.

# Everything Under Control... Well Almost!

Taking the various points I have talked about in this book into account, I have made a Corporate Wife Checklist for you to consider.

- When attending in your capacity as Corporate Wife, your role is to support your professional partner.

- Recognise your role as a skill, and one that you can take pride in delivering.

- Observe the title of Corporate Wife in relation to what it means to you, and not what it means to others.

- Know that the corporate networking environment is crucial to your husband's success, and the other professionals alongside him.

- Make the necessary arrangements in your personal life with regard to home and work commitments, so you can give the corporate event the time and attention it requires from you.

- Step out of your comfort zone, as it will enable you to experience different venues, enjoy different events and meet a variety of people.

- Take "just in case" items in your handbag, to allow for any unexpected situations.

- Smile, make eye contact, show your friendly, approachable demeanour.

- Make the effort with small talk to develop conversation and rapport.

- Listen to others. Remember comments made by others to build conversations later on.

- Do not dominate conversations. A corporate networking event is not your platform to make your voice heard.

- Show gratitude when attending an event as a corporate guest.

- Give outsider information to your husband – your observations may assist his professional understanding of those he is working alongside.

- Do not respond to negative behaviour. It is not the environment in which to give your personal opinion. Be mindful that it is your husband's working environment.

**My mistakes:** I have made plenty of mistakes in my role of Corporate Wife, mainly in the early days. My walk of shame is as follows:

Attending an event, I was wearing clothing not particularly suitable for a Corporate Wife – it was figure hugging and therefore uncomfortable for many hours of sitting down, and showed a bit of cleavage which the Creep naturally made loud comments about. I was also wearing high heeled shoes which matched the outfit in colour, so was a "vision" in blood red, but they were a little too high for me to walk elegantly in, especially after I'd been sitting still for a long period of time.

> *The Remedy: wear clothes and shoes that complement the occasion and do not cause you any discomfort or unwanted attention.*

A client, whilst at a relaxed social event, asked me whether my husband was busy. I confirmed that to be the case, whereupon the client asked if the workload was of any particular interest. He then asked if my husband did much for a particular company, and I confirmed that he did. The following day, the client contacted my husband and asked if he was working on a deal that had been awarded to that client's competitor. My husband was, and it had. The client had – in the guise of small talk – been fishing for information when he spoke to me. Fortunately, I had not divulged anything of a confidential nature, so that was the first and last time I was ever *nearly* caught out.

> *The Remedy: be mindful that however friendly an interaction may be, you are still in attendance because of the working relationship. Do not discuss specific business relationships or disclose any details regarding your husband's work connections.*

Attending a corporate dinner, I took too big a bite of a crusty bread roll as the host was mid-sentence. Some crumbs went down the wrong way, causing me to splutter and gasp and generally make a complete racket, then rush through the restaurant, eyes streaming, to escape to the Ladies. Some time later, I attempted to glide back to the table in a ladylike fashion as if nothing had happened, with a stinging throat, the remnants of mascara clinging on to my eyelashes, and my cheeks flushed from the shock and embarrassment.

> *The Remedy: take small bites of food, perhaps with a sip of water. Or better still, don't sneak a bite of food when the host is holding court.*

On attending a Partners' Conference, we wives decided to stay up later than our husbands, even though we'd been attending separate events and had no idea when the corporate event would finish. I impressed myself by staying out until 4am, then had to give up and head to bed. Our hotel room was near the lifts, and as I prepared to get into bed, I heard the ping of the lift doors opening. I raced to the door and peered through the spy hole, preparing to jump out and scare my husband (which I thought would be extremely funny). Instead I found myself spying on a colleague who was guiding a "lady of the night" into his room.

*The Remedy: go to bed at 9pm, with ear plugs.*

Hosting a dinner party at home for some clients and their wives, Andrew and I decided on delicious beef and stilton parcels that we had eaten previously. The hungry guests were awaiting the meal, so we carefully guided the parcels off the baking tray onto our best Wedgwood plates, only to discover that the butcher had sold us Cornish pasties by mistake.

*The Remedy: if you want to impress, check what you are buying, then check again.*

Attending a Partners' Conference, I spent an entertaining evening in the company of other wives and partners, swapping funny stories. We got on to the subject of late night programmes, and I decided in my wisdom to share details about a programme I had seen where couples discussed their more unusual sexual practices. Thank goodness I also relayed the story to my husband, as at breakfast the next morning at least five of his colleagues made personal enquiries of us, based upon the detail I had shared the night before.

*The Remedy: remember that you are on duty as a Corporate Wife. Regardless of the hour and the level of alcohol being consumed, some people will recall the topics of conversations.*

# And Finally

An assistant at a law firm was co-hosting a dinner event. His wife was running late, keeping the entire group waiting, and he could not get through to her on her mobile phone.

She finally charged into the restaurant, barking loudly at her husband that he had no idea how difficult it was sorting out the children and trying to "glam up" in time for the event. She then went on to introduce herself to the attending clients and their wives, all the while verbally dismissing her husband's colleagues and spouses.

When she was introduced to the senior gentleman from the client company, she expressed how he should give her husband all his biggest deals as she had her eye on a particular handbag that she wanted for Christmas. Then she cackled loudly, looking around for approval for her humour as the entire group sat quietly, watching her in action.

Then she went to the Ladies.

Now, if that story didn't bring a smile to your face, may I humbly request you go back to the beginning of this handbook and start again.

xxx

# About the Author

Sarah Watson has been married to Andrew, a solicitor, for more than 20 years and has worked as a legal secretary for more than 25 years.

After observing how people respond in different ways to the corporate networking environment, Sarah came to the conclusion that there is a correct code of conduct for Corporate Wives to recognise and demonstrate, and that is what persuaded her to write this handbook.

When Sarah is not on duty as a Corporate Wife, she can be found either working as a legal secretary, carrying out her voluntary duties, or pretending to catch up with household chores.

Free time includes walking the family dog in the Surrey Hills, catching up with family, meeting friends, or relaxing with a cup of tea.

**Email:** info@thecwclub.com
**Facebook:** @thecwclub
**Twitter:** @SWtheCWclub
**Instagram:** sarahwcw
**Blog:** thecwclub.com